Higher

German

Leckie×Leckie

First exam published in 2004.
Published by Leckie & Leckie Ltd, 3rd Floor, 4 Queen Street, Edinburgh EH2 1JE
tel: 0131 220 6831 fax: 0131 225 9987 enquiries@leckieandleckie.co.uk www.leckieandleckie.co.uk

ISBN 978-1-84372-555-8

A CIP Catalogue record for this book is available from the British Library.

Printed in Scotland by Scotprint.

Leckie & Leckie is a division of Huveaux plc.

Leckie & Leckie is grateful to the copyright holders, as credited at the back of the book, for permission to use their material. Every effort has been made to trace the copyright holders and to obtain their permission for the use of copyright material. Leckie & Leckie will gladly receive information enabling them to rectify any error or omission in subsequent editions.

2004 | Higher

[BLANK]

X060/301

| NATIONAL QUALIFICATIONS 2004 | TUESDAY, 18 MAY 9.00 AM – 10.40 AM | GERMAN HIGHER Reading and Directed Writing |

45 marks are allocated to this paper. The value attached to each question is shown in the margin after each question.

You should spend approximately one hour on Section I and 40 minutes on Section II.

You may use a German dictionary.

SCOTTISH QUALIFICATIONS AUTHORITY ©

SECTION I—READING

Read this magazine article carefully and answer **in English** the questions which follow it.

The article deals with a girl who has changed jobs five times in the last seven years.

Job-Hopping

Ein Leben lang denselben Beruf? „Nichts für mich!", sagt Mona. In den letzten sieben Jahren hat sie fünfmal den Job gewechselt. Man könnte auch sagen: Mona ist eine Job-Hopperin.

Wie viele Schulabgänger weiß Mona nicht recht, welcher Beruf ihr Spaß machen könnte. Ihr Vater ist Steuerberater und hofft, dass die Tochter seinem Vorbild folgt. Mona ist nahe daran, sich an
5 der Uni einzuschreiben. Doch sie zögert. Als ihr ein Freund anbietet, in seinem Möbelgeschäft zu arbeiten, sagt sie sofort zu. So wird diese Arbeit als Verkäuferin ihr Job Nummer eins.

Sie beschließt von nun an, sich die Zeit zu
10 nehmen, um durch Praktika und Jobs in verschiedene Bereiche hineinzuschnuppern. Dadurch kann sie sich und ihre Talente austesten.

Nach sechs Monaten kündigt sie und reist durch Mittelamerika. Dort wird ihr klar, dass sie Zahlen
15 und Bilanzen, kurz: BWL*, nicht mag. Ein Sprachenstudium, überlegt sie, das lässt noch alles offen. Gedacht, gemacht: Sie reist heim, schreibt sich an der Kölner Uni ein und beginnt, Französisch und Spanisch zu studieren.

20 Als Nebenjob sucht sie sich eine Arbeit, die ihr Einblick in ein neues Metier gibt: die Medien. „Eine aufregende Branche, in der wahnsinnig viel passiert. Ich wollte gucken, ob das was für mich ist." Beim Fernsehsender *Vox* bekommt sie ihren
25 Job Nummer zwei. Doch vorrangig widmet sich Mona dem Studium. Aber je weiter sie kommt, desto deutlicher spürt sie, dass sie zu viele Probleme mit der Grammatik hat, um erfolgreich weiterzustudieren. Darum bricht sie nach drei
30 Semestern die Uni ab.

Mona bittet ihre Freundin Astrid um Rat. Die beiden brainstormen: Was soll Mona machen? „Was Praktisches", bestimmt Astrid, während sie in einer Zeitschrift blättert. Plötzlich springt ihr
35 eine Anzeige ins Auge: Flugbegleiterinnen gesucht. Viel unterwegs sein, fremde Länder sehen, ständig Neues erleben, mit Menschen zu tun haben. Mona bewirbt sich um Job Nummer drei. Und wird genommen. Ihre Eltern sind
40 wenig begeistert. Doch letztlich vertrauen sie der Wahl ihrer Tochter.

Mona nutzt die Zeit bis zu ihrem ersten Flug für ihr viertes Jobexperiment. Sie verkauft Kinderkleidung in einem Kaufhaus. Was sie vor allem dort lernt, ist Teamarbeit - mit anderen 45 Hand in Hand zu arbeiten. Das war für sie eine sehr wichtige Erfahrung.

Als Flugbegleiterin lernt sie die Welt kennen. Am besten gefällt ihr Südafrika. Nach drei Jahren Fliegerei zieht sie Bilanz. Sie hat viele 50 Länder gesehen, ihre Fremdsprachen verbessert, ist flexibler geworden und weiß, was guter Service bedeutet. „Aus diesem Beruf kann man mehr nicht rausholen." Also: Was Neues anfangen. 55

Jetzt will sie das Schreiben ausprobieren. Sie bewirbt sich erfolgreich um ein Praktikum bei einer Fachzeitschrift in *Köln*. Wie immer, wenn sie von etwas begeistert ist, arbeitet Mona extrem engagiert. Ergebnis: Nach vier Monaten 60 Praktikum bekommt sie eine feste Stelle—Job Nummer fünf.

Die Hamburger S-Bahn bestimmt ihr weiteres Schicksal. Mona ist auf dem Weg zu Freunden, als sie im Waggon einen Aufkleber sieht. Der 65 wirbt für das Studium „Mode-Journalismus" an einer privaten Schule. Journalismus ist gut, denkt Mona, Modejournalismus ist besser. Sie ruft die Nummer an und ist sofort begeistert: „Marketing, PR, Italienisch, das Studienangebot gefiel mir." 70 Mona zieht also um nach *Hamburg*. Und die Freunde aus der Schulzeit sind noch weiter weg. Aber: „Ich telefoniere viel. Tiefe Freundschaften halten auch auf Distanz, glaube ich. Genauso wie die gute Beziehung zu meinen Eltern." 75

Mittlerweile weiß Mona, was sie will: „Ich brauche keine Sicherheit. Mein Ziel im Leben ist es, glücklich zu sein." Und wie sieht es mit Geld aus? Kein Problem für Mona: „Reich muss ich nicht sein, da ich sowieso keine Familie gründen 80 möchte."

Trotz der vielen Jobwechsel ist Mona „innerlich ruhiger geworden". Immerhin kann sie sich jetzt vorstellen, als Journalistin den Beruf
85 gefunden zu haben, der ihr auf lange Sicht Spaß macht. „Diese Ausbildung ziehe ich durch. Bestimmt!" Sie lächelt. „Aber ein Café zu eröffnen, könnte ich mir auch vorstellen."

*BWL = business management

QUESTIONS

Marks

1. (a) What hope did Mona's father have for her future? **1 point**

   (b) Why did Mona eventually decide not to go to university? **1 point**

2. Read paragraph 2 (lines 9–12).

   From this point on, what did Mona decide to do? **2 points**

3. Read paragraph 3 (lines 13–19).

   What conclusion did Mona come to six months later? **2 points**

4. Now read paragraph 4 (lines 20–30).

   (a) Why did Mona decide to try a job in the media? **1 point**

   (b) Why did she give up her university course? **1 point**

5. Read paragraph 5 (lines 31–41).

   (a) What attracted Mona to becoming an air hostess? **2 points**

   (b) How did her parents react to job number three? **1 point**

6. Read paragraph 7 (lines 48–55).

   After three years, Mona took stock of her career to date.

   (a) What factors did she consider? **2 points**

   (b) What conclusion did she reach? **1 point**

7. Read paragraphs 8 and 9 (lines 56–75).

   (a) What was the result of Mona's work experience at a magazine publisher's? **1 point**

   (b) Mona then moved to Hamburg for her next job. How does she cope with being so far from friends and family? **2 points**

8. Read the final two paragraphs (lines 76–88).

   (a) What is Mona's attitude to money? **1 point**

   (b) How does she see her future now? **2 points**

(20 points)

= 20 marks

9. Translate into English:

   „Mona nutzt die Zeit . . . eine sehr wichtige Erfahrung." (lines 42–47) **10**

(30)

[Turn over for SECTION II on *Page four*

SECTION II—DIRECTED WRITING

Marks

Your school/college has established links and an exchange programme with a school/college in Germany. You took part in the first exchange in April of this year, when you stayed with the family of one of the German students and attended school/college.

On your return you are asked to write a report **in German** for inclusion in the foreign language section of your school/college magazine.

You must include the following information and **you should try to add** other relevant details:

- where the family lived and what their home was like

- where the school/college was situated and what it was like

- what was different about school/college in Germany

- what you did in the intervals

- what activities were organised for your group when you were not in school/college

- how you coped with living away from home with a German family.

Your report should be 150 – 180 words in length.

Marks will be deducted for any area of information that is omitted.

(15)

[END OF QUESTION PAPER]

X060/303

NATIONAL
QUALIFICATIONS
2004

TUESDAY, 18 MAY
11.00 AM – 12.00 NOON

GERMAN
HIGHER
Listening Transcript

This paper must not be seen by any candidate.

The material overleaf is provided for use in an emergency only (eg the recording or equipment proving faulty) or where permission has been given in advance by SQA for the material to be read to candidates with special needs. The material must be read exactly as printed.

SCOTTISH
QUALIFICATIONS
AUTHORITY

> **Instructions to reader(s):**
> The dialogue below should be read in approximately 4 minutes. On completion of the first reading, pause for two minutes, then read the dialogue a second time.
>
> Where special arrangements have been agreed in advance to allow the reading of the material, those sections marked **(m)** should be read by a male speaker and those marked **(f)** by a female.

Lisa, a German girl from Stuttgart on holiday in Scotland, is interviewed about what she does outside school.

(m)   **Als Schülerin hast du bestimmt nicht so viel Freizeit. Aber hast du auch irgendwann einen Nebenjob gehabt?**

(f)   Ja. Ich habe jetzt in der elften Klasse einen Nebenjob angenommen. Anfangs bin ich zweimal die Woche zu einer Familie gegangen. Die Mutter ist in der Woche alleine, weil der Vater in Frankfurt arbeiten muss. Und sie hat drei kleine Kinder. Das Kleinste war gerade fünf Monate alt, als ich dort angefangen habe, und da hab' ich ihr dann geholfen.

(m)   **Wie hast du der Mutter geholfen?**

(f)   Ich habe zuerst mit den Kindern gespielt und dann mit dem Essen geholfen. Ich musste auch die Kinder baden und dann habe ich sie ins Bett gebracht.

(m)   **Und das Baby gewickelt, oder?**

(f)   Ja, auch das Baby gewickelt. Und die Andere, die schon zwei Jahre alt war, als ich angefangen habe, die musste ich auch wickeln.

(m)   **Wie viel bekommst du pro Stunde?**

(f)   Ich verdiene pro Stunde fünf Euro.

(m)   **Ist das normal für diese Art von Arbeit?**

(f)   Also, ich bin jetzt bei mehreren Familien, wo ich babysitten gehe und da habe ich überall den festen Preis von fünf Euro ausgemacht.

(m)   **Bekommst du also kein Geld mehr von deinen Eltern?**

(f)   Doch, ich bekomme von meinen Eltern immer noch Taschengeld. Ich bekomme es monatlich. Ich bekomme dreißig Euro auf mein Bankkonto überwiesen und fünfzehn Euro kriege ich so.

(m)   **Musst du deine Kleider selbst kaufen?**

(f)   Nee, von meinem Taschengeld brauche ich keine Kleidung und Schulsachen zu kaufen. Und wenn ich ausgehe, dann bekomme ich manchmal noch Geld dazu, besonders zum Essen, oder wenn ich ins Kino gehe.

(m)   **Man liest ja, dass junge Leute oft noch Geld dazu bekommen, zum Beispiel von den Großeltern. Ist das bei dir auch der Fall?**

(f)   Nee, leider nicht, weil meine Verwandtschaft weiter weg wohnt.

(m)   **Was machst du gern in der Freizeit?**

(f)   Also, ich spiele Basketball in einem Verein und ich sollte dreimal in der Woche trainieren. Aber während der Schulzeit schaffe ich es meistens nur einmal die Woche. Und während der Saison habe ich auch Spiele gegen andere Vereine. Sonst gehe ich gern mit meinen Freunden weg. Unter der Woche eher seltener aber am Wochenende dann in Bars, Cafés und Discos. Man muss allerdings einen haben, der fahren kann, weil man sonst den Bus nehmen muss. Es gibt auch Sammeltaxis bei uns; die kann man anrufen und bestellen. Das ist doch ganz praktisch, weil sie auch bis nach Hause fahren. Und das letzte fährt um zehn nach eins. Weil ich auch mit dem Bus in die Schule fahre, habe ich einen Buspass. Mit dem Buspass ist das Sammeltaxi dann billiger; ich glaub, es kostet einen Euro zwanzig.

(m)   **Wie wichtig ist für dich der Computer?**

(f)   Also, auf der einen Seite kann ich durch E-mails Kontakt mit meinen Freunden in Florida und Australien halten. Und als meine Schwester ein Jahr lang in Italien arbeitete, haben wir uns jeden Abend gemailt. Es lohnt sich auch jetzt noch, wo ich gerade in Schottland bin, da ich meine Familie mailen kann. Sonst benutze ich den Computer für die Schule, um Referate zu schreiben oder um Sachen im Internet zu finden, Informationen über bestimmte Themen, zum Beispiel. Aber Computerspiele spiele ich eigentlich gar nicht.

(m)   **Hast du einen eigenen Computer zu Hause?**

(f)   Wir haben einen zusammen für die Familie. Das reicht. Da ich eben keine Computerspiele mag, ist der Computer eigentlich immer dann frei, wenn ihn einer für die Schule braucht.

[END OF TRANSCRIPT]

[BLANK PAGE]

FOR OFFICIAL USE

Examiner's Marks	
A	
B	

Total Mark

X060/302

NATIONAL
QUALIFICATIONS
2004

TUESDAY, 18 MAY
11.00 AM – 12.00 NOON

GERMAN
HIGHER
Listening/Writing

Fill in these boxes and read what is printed below.

Full name of centre

Town

Forename(s)

Surname

Date of birth
Day Month Year   Scottish candidate number   Number of seat

Do not open this paper until told to do so.

Answer Section A **in English** and Section B **in German**.

Section A

Listen carefully to the recording with a view to answering, **in English**, the questions printed in this answer book. Write your answers **clearly** and **legibly** in the spaces provided after each question.

You will have 2 minutes to study the questions before hearing the recording.

The recording will be played **twice**, with an interval of 2 minutes between the two playings.

You may make notes at any time but only in this answer book. **Draw your pen through any notes before you hand in the book.**

Move on to Section B when you have completed Section A: you will **not** be told when to do this.

Section B

Do not write your response in this book: use the **4 page lined answer sheet**.

You will be told to insert the answer sheet inside this book before handing in your work.

You may consult a German dictionary at any time during **both** sections.

Before leaving the examination room you must give this book to the invigilator. If you do not, you may lose all the marks for this paper.

SCOTTISH
QUALIFICATIONS
AUTHORITY

©

Section A

Marks

Lisa, a German girl from Stuttgart on holiday in Scotland, is interviewed about what she does outside school.

1. (*a*) How often did Lisa do her part-time job, helping in a family?

1 point

    (*b*) Why was her help needed?

2 points

2. (*a*) What exactly did this job involve? Mention **two** things.

2 points

    (*b*) How much was Lisa paid for her work?

1 point

3. What does Lisa say about pocket money?

2 points

4. (*a*) What does Lisa not have to use her pocket money for?

1 point

    (*b*) When do her parents give her extra money?

1 point

Marks

4. (continued)

    (*c*) Why does she not get any extra money from relatives?   **1 point**

5.   What role does sport play in Lisa's life?   **2 points**

6.   (*a*) What advantages do the "Sammeltaxis" have, when Lisa is out with friends?   **2 points**

    (*b*) What benefit does Lisa gain from having a school bus pass?   **1 point**

7.   (*a*) How does Lisa use computers to keep in touch with other people? Give **two** specific examples of this.   **2 points**

    (*b*) Why is one computer enough for Lisa's family?   **2 points**

(20 points)

= 20 marks

[Turn over for Section B on *Page four*

Marks

Section B

Und du? Spielt der Computer eine wichtige Rolle in deinem Leben? Was machst du sonst in deiner Freizeit? Woher bekommst du das Geld dafür?

Schreibe 120 – 150 Worte zu diesen Fragen!

10

(30)

USE THE 4 PAGE LINED ANSWER SHEET FOR YOUR ANSWER TO SECTION B

[END OF QUESTION PAPER]

2005 | Higher

[BLANK PAGE]

X060/301

NATIONAL
QUALIFICATIONS
2005

FRIDAY, 27 MAY
9.00 AM – 10.40 AM

GERMAN
HIGHER
Reading and
Directed Writing

45 marks are allocated to this paper. The value attached to each question is shown in the margin after each question.

You should spend approximately one hour on Section I and 40 minutes on Section II.

You may use a German dictionary.

Read this magazine article carefully then answer **in English** the questions which follow it.

This article deals with a girl who has become a shopaholic.

Maria, 18: „Ich bin shopping-süchtig!"

Durch die Einkaufsstraßen schlendern, Klamotten anprobieren, sich etwas Cooles kaufen—für die meisten Teenager ist das einfach nur Freizeit-Fun. Doch für Maria
5 ist es viel mehr: Beim Shoppen fühlt sie sich wie ein Star, für den ein roter Teppich ausgerollt wird. Ihre Augen beginnen unnatürlich zu glänzen, ihr Herz schlägt schneller, sie hat Schmetterlinge im
10 Bauch—und will nur noch eins: kaufen!

„Es ist wie ein Anfall", erzählt Maria. „Immer das Gleiche: Ich sehe Popsängerinnen im TV—und sofort will ich auch so coole Klamotten haben wie sie!" So
15 will Maria auch aussehen—und der einzige Weg dorthin führt für sie durch die Shops der Einkaufszentren: „Eine Stimme in meinem Kopf sagt „Kauf dir das!" Und dann kann ich nicht anders. Ich will auch
20 schön sein, attraktiv und beliebt!"

Mit 13 Jahren war es noch ganz harmlos: Maria ging mit Freundinnen shoppen—wie Tausende anderer Girls. „Aber dann fingen die anderen an, über mich zu lästern und
25 Witze zu machen, weil ich immer massenhaft Einkaufstüten nach Hause schleppte—viel mehr als sie!" Maria zieht sich von ihrer Clique zurück, sie wird einsam.

Maria kann mit 50 Euro Taschengeld ihre
30 Einkaufssucht nicht finanzieren. Aber sie findet andere Quellen: Sie bekommt von den Großeltern immer wieder etwas zugesteckt. „Ich hab mir auch oft was geliehen und es gab Krach, weil ich es nicht zurückgezahlt,
35 sondern immer mehr gekauft habe. Zu Weihnachten oder zum Geburtstag wünschte ich mir von der Familie Geld—und bekam es auch." Schließlich beginnt Maria sogar ihr Sparkonto zu plündern!

40 „Mit 17 Jahren verdiente ich zum ersten Mal selbst etwas, rund 400 Euro im Monat. Und jetzt ging es erst richtig los, denn je mehr ich hatte, desto mehr gab ich aus! Meine Eltern meinten, dass es gut ist, wenn

ihre Tochter lernt, mit Geld umzugehen und 45 mischten sich nicht ein."

Und dann entdeckte Maria das Internet! Aussuchen, bestellen—und irgendwann zahlen. „Manchmal hatte ich keine Ahnung mehr, wie viel Geld ich schon ausgegeben 50 hatte." Die Geldsorgen bedrücken Maria immer stärker. Sie verbringt schlaflose Nächte. „Ich sah mich mit hohen Schulden, ohne die Möglichkeit, ein ganz normales Leben zu führen. Aber trotzdem konnte ich 55 das Shopping einfach nicht aufgeben."

Maria macht zwar Versuche, von ihrer Kaufsucht loszukommen. „Ich verordnete mir selbst ein „Stadtverbot" oder ging los, ohne Geld mitzunehmen. Doch dann stand 60 ich vor den bunt dekorierten Schaufenstern und schrieb Listen mit all den Dingen, die ich mir kaufen würde, sobald ich wieder Geld dabei hätte!"

Aber das tolle Gefühl beim Einkaufen 65 dauert nicht lange; wie bei einer Drogensucht braucht Maria immer höhere Dosen, kauft immer mehr, immer schneller. Und dann sitzt sie zu Hause auf ihrem Bett und weiß: Nichts hat sie durch ihre Einkäufe 70 geändert, gar nichts! „Ich brach immer häufiger ganz plötzlich in Tränen aus, wurde nervös, fing an zu zittern und konnte mich schließlich kaum noch konzentrieren." Marias Eltern sind vollkommen ratlos. Ist 75 ihre Tochter vielleicht krank?

„Meine Eltern haben mir gesagt, ich sollte zum Arzt. Und das war das Beste, was mir passieren konnte! Der Arzt hat lange mit mir geredet. Zum ersten Mal habe ich ganz offen 80 von meiner Shoppingsucht gesprochen. Ich habe zugegeben, wie unglücklich ich war."

„Der Arzt hat für mich dann den Kontakt zu einem Therapeuten gemacht, der sich mit dem Problem Kaufsucht auskennt. Vor zwei 85 Wochen hatte ich schon meine erste Sitzung bei ihm. Ich habe auch schon ein paar Erfolge zu verbuchen: Ich leihe mir kein

90 Geld mehr von meinen Freunden und habe ihnen schon fast alles zurückgezahlt. Aber das ist nur ein Anfang. Es ist noch zu früh, um etwas darüber zu sagen, wann ich in ein Geschäft gehen werde, ohne die Regale leer zu kaufen. Ich will es aber schaffen und endlich ein ganz normales Leben führen." 95

QUESTIONS

Marks

1. What effect does shopping have on Maria? **2 points**

2. Read lines 11–20.

   Why does Maria feel a constant need to shop? **2 points**

3. Read lines 21–28.

   How did Maria's addiction affect her relationship with her friends? **1 point**

4. Now read lines 29–39.

   Maria's pocket money is not enough to pay for her addiction. How did she finance her shopping sprees before she got a job? **3 points**

5. Read lines 40–46.

   (*a*) What happened when she started to earn money for the first time? **1 point**

   (*b*) Why did her parents not interfere? **1 point**

6. Read lines 47–56.

   (*a*) What does Maria say, which shows that her spending was out of control? **1 point**

   (*b*) How did Maria's money worries affect her? **3 points**

7. Read lines 57–64.

   (*a*) How did Maria try to cure her addiction? **1 point**

   (*b*) What shows that this did not work? **1 point**

8. Read lines 65–76.

   Why did Maria's parents end up wondering if she might be ill? **2 points**

9. Read lines 83–95.

   What success has she had, since seeing a therapist? **2 points**

   (20 points)

   = 20 marks

10. Translate into English:

   „Meine Eltern haben mir gesagt . . . wie unglücklich ich war." (lines 77–82) **10**

   (30)

   [Turn over for SECTION II on *Page four*

SECTION II—DIRECTED WRITING

Marks

Recently you did work experience in a German-speaking country. You have to write a report for the languages department in your school/college.

You must include the following information and **you should try to add** other relevant details:

- how you travelled and what you did during the journey

- what the job was and what hours you worked

- how you got on with your co-workers and what you liked/disliked about them

- what you did in the evenings

- what the local area was like

- what you got out of the experience.

Your report should be 150 – 180 words in length.

Marks will be deducted for any area of information that is omitted. (15)

[END OF QUESTION PAPER]

X060/303

NATIONAL
QUALIFICATIONS
2005

FRIDAY, 27 MAY
11.00 AM – 12.00 NOON

GERMAN
HIGHER
Listening Transcript

This paper must not be seen by any candidate.

The material overleaf is provided for use in an emergency only (eg the recording or equipment proving faulty) or where permission has been given in advance by SQA for the material to be read to candidates with special needs. The material must be read exactly as printed.

SCOTTISH
QUALIFICATIONS
AUTHORITY

Daniel, a 16-year-old German boy, is interviewed about his sporting activities and how they might clash with his love life.

(f)   **Was machst du im Sportbereich?**

(m)   Ich bin Torwart in einer Hockeymannschaft und zweimal pro Woche gehe ich zum Training. Wir haben auch ein- oder zweimal die Woche ein Spiel und jedes zweite Wochenende gibt es auch ein Auswärtsspiel irgendwoanders im Land, und das nimmt viel Zeit in Anspruch.

(f)   **Gibt es dann Probleme mit deiner Freundin, weil du so viel Sport treibst?**

(m)   Ja. Ich habe zwar keine Freundin, aber ich würde meine Mannschaft für kein Mädchen im Stich lassen. Sport ist mir sehr wichtig.

(f)   **Was meinst du, kommt ein sportlicher Junge bei Mädchen besser an?**

(m)   Hmm. Ich glaube, ja. Mädchen achten sehr auf das Aussehen von Jungs und finden es gut, wenn ein Junge eine sportliche Figur hat. Viele sagen zwar, Äußerlichkeiten seien nicht wichtig, aber ein dicker Freund ist vielen Mädchen dann doch peinlich.

(f)   **Interessierst du dich auch außerhalb des Trainings für Sport?**

(m)   Klar. Im Fernsehen gucke ich mir Sportsendungen an. Meine Lieblingssendung, „ran", sehe ich jeden Samstag. Ich lese auch regelmäßig Sportzeitschriften und, wenn ich Zeit habe, spiele ich mit meinem Bruder Tischtennis.

(f)   **Wenn du so viel Zeit für Sport aufbringst—wo und wann willst du dann ein Mädchen kennen lernen?**

(m)   Hmm. Das ist in der Tat nicht so einfach. Da ich jetzt 16 bin, hoffe ich, dass ich abends öfter weggehen darf. Ich denke, dass man beim Tanzen oder im Eiscafé gut Mädchen kennen lernen kann.

(f)   **Angenommen, du bist frisch verliebt und du musst zwischen Freundin und Training entscheiden. Was würdest du machen?**

(m)   Ah. Es würde mir schon schwer fallen, aber ich denke, Training und Turnier gehen vor. Ich bin der einzige Torwart und deshalb für die Mannschaft verantwortlich. Und eigentlich erwarte ich von meiner Freundin, dass sie das versteht.

(f)   **Wärst du denn überhaupt bereit, dein Training wegen eines Mädchens einzuschränken?**

(m)   Ich wäre zu einem Kompromiss bereit: Alle zwei Wochen lasse ich einmal das Training ausfallen. Das gilt aber nur, wenn die Freundin ihr Hobby auch einschränkt. Beide müssen etwas aufgeben.

(f)   **Muss ein Mädchen sportlich sein, damit sie dich interessiert?**

(m)   Nicht unbedingt, aber ein Pluspunkt wäre es schon. Vielleicht würde sie mich dann eher verstehen, wenn ich am Wochenende mal keine Zeit habe. Toll wäre es, wenn sie sich ab und zu ein Spiel unserer Mannschaft anschauen würde.

(f)   Wie oft würdest du denn deine Freundin überhaupt sehen wollen?

(m)   Nicht mehr als zweimal in der Woche—und natürlich am Samstagabend.

(f)   Nicht öfter?

(m)   Nein. Viele Pärchen in meinem Freundeskreis treffen sich täglich. Das finde ich nicht okay. Sie vergessen alles um sich herum. Meiner Meinung nach sollte man nicht die Freunde und die Mannschaft wegen einer Beziehung im Stich lassen.

[END OF TRANSCRIPT]

[BLANK PAGE]

FOR OFFICIAL USE

Total Mark

X060/302

NATIONAL
QUALIFICATIONS
2005

FRIDAY, 27 MAY
11.00 AM – 12.00 NOON

GERMAN
HIGHER
Listening/Writing

Fill in these boxes and read what is printed below.

Full name of centre

Town

Forename(s)

Surname

Date of birth

| Day | Month | Year | | Scottish candidate number | | Number of seat |

Do not open this paper until told to do so.

Answer Section A **in English** and Section B **in German**.

Section A

Listen carefully to the recording with a view to answering, **in English**, the questions printed in this answer book. Write your answers **clearly** and **legibly** in the spaces provided after each question.

You will have 2 minutes to study the questions before hearing the recording.

The recording will be played **twice**, with an interval of 2 minutes between the two playings.

You may make notes at any time but only in this answer book. **Draw your pen through any notes before you hand in the book.**

Move on to Section B when you have completed Section A: you will **not** be told when to do this.

Section B

Do not write your response in this book: use the 4 page lined answer sheet.

You will be told to insert the answer sheet inside this book before handing in your work.

You may consult a German dictionary at any time during **both** sections.

Before leaving the examination room you must give this book to the invigilator. If you do not, you may lose all the marks for this paper.

SCOTTISH
QUALIFICATIONS
AUTHORITY

©

Section A

Marks

Daniel, a 16-year-old German boy, is interviewed about his sporting activities and how they might clash with his love life.

1. (*a*) What demands does hockey make on Daniel's time each week?

2 points

(*b*) How often does he have a match somewhere else in the region?

1 point

2. Why does Daniel think that boys who are into sport find it easier to attract a girlfriend?

2 points

3. What interest does Daniel take in sport, apart from his hockey?

2 points

4. (*a*) What is going to change, now that he is 16?

1 point

(*b*) Where does he think he might find a girlfriend?

1 point

5. If Daniel had to choose between going to training and going out with his girlfriend, why would he go to training?

1 point

Marks

6. (*a*) What compromise would Daniel be prepared to make, if he had a girlfriend?

2 points

(*b*) What would he expect the girl to do in return?

1 point

7. Why does Daniel think that having a girlfriend who is interested in sport might be a good thing?

2 points

8. When would Daniel want to see his girlfriend?

2 points

9. (*a*) How often do some of the couples he knows see each other?

1 point

(*b*) Why does he not approve of this?

2 points

(20 points)

= 20 marks

[Turn over for Section B on *Page four*

Marks

Section B

Für Daniel ist Sport sehr wichtig. Was ist für dich sehr wichtig? Musst du zwischen Freund/Freundin und anderen Interessen entscheiden? Wie kommst du denn zurecht?

Schreibe 120 – 150 Worte zu diesen Fragen!

10

(30)

USE THE 4 PAGE LINED ANSWER SHEET FOR YOUR ANSWER TO SECTION B

[END OF QUESTION PAPER]

[BLANK PAGE]

X060/301

| NATIONAL QUALIFICATIONS 2006 | WEDNESDAY, 24 MAY 9.00 AM – 10.40 AM | GERMAN HIGHER Reading and Directed Writing |

45 marks are allocated to this paper. The value attached to each question is shown after each question.

You should spend approximately one hour on Section I and 40 minutes on Section II.

You may use a German dictionary.

SCOTTISH QUALIFICATIONS AUTHORITY

Read this magazine article carefully then answer **in English** the questions which follow it.

This article deals with school students in Hersbruck (Bavaria) who have part-time jobs.

Für Handy, Klamotten, Kino, Urlaub

Schüler bessern sich durch Jobs ihr Taschengeld auf—Die Schulleistung darf nicht darunter leiden.

Handy, Klamotten, Kino und Urlaub—das Leben eines Schülers kann ganz schön teuer werden. Dafür reicht das Taschengeld meist nicht aus, das wissen viele Jugendliche aus
5 leidvoller Erfahrung. Ferienjobs sind für sie deshalb eine willkommene Alternative zum elterlichen Geldbeutel. Mittlerweile gibt es aber zahlreiche Schüler, die nicht nur in den Ferien, sondern regelmäßig neben der
10 Schule arbeiten, um ihr eigenes Geld zu verdienen.

Einer von ihnen ist Sebastian Herbst. Zweimal pro Woche schwingt er sich in den Fahrradsattel, um Fernsehzeitschriften und
15 Illustrierte auszutragen. Seit zwei Jahren verschafft sich der 17-Jährige, der in die zehnte Klasse des Paul-Pfinzing-Gymnasiums geht, damit ein Stück finanzieller Unabhängigkeit von seinen
20 Eltern.

Das verdiente Geld gibt er hauptsächlich für Handy und Klamotten aus. Auch den Schüleraustausch nach Frankreich und die diesjährige Reise nach Schottland will er
25 damit bezahlen. Dass er den Job überhaupt bekommen hat, hat Sebastian eigentlich seiner Mutter zu verdanken, die damals in der Zeitung die Stellenanzeige las.

Die Arbeit selbst ist für ihn mittlerweile
30 zur reinen Routine geworden. So hat er sich den Bezirk, für den er zuständig ist, in drei Touren eingeteilt, die er dann nacheinander mit dem Fahrrad abfährt. Bei jedem Wetter natürlich, denn die Kunden wollen ihre
35 abonnierten Zeitschriften ja auch rechtzeitig erhalten. „Man muss sich an die Zeiten und Termine halten", sagt Sebastian. „Aber wenn es heiß ist oder wenn Glatteis ist, ist es schon blöd", gesteht er lächelnd: „Der Job
40 macht mir viel Spaß; es ist immerhin leicht verdientes Geld und meine Schularbeit leidet ja auch nicht darunter."

Finanzielle Unabhängigkeit war auch das Ziel von Susanne Hupfer. Früher jobbte sie gelegentlich als Babysitterin, seit längerem 45 bedient die 17-jährige Realschülerin nun aber schon im Café Corretto. Im Laden sah sie vor zwei Jahren das Stellengesuch aushängen, bewarb sich und nach einem Probearbeitstag hatte sie den Job. „Ein 50 Grund, warum ich unbedingt kellnern wollte, ist, weil zu dem Stundenlohn auch noch das Trinkgeld dazukommt", erklärt sie. „Zudem ist die Arbeit äußerst abwechslungsreich, denn jeder Gast ist 55 schließlich anders. Der Umgang mit den Menschen fällt mir aber leicht. Man lernt schnell, locker auf die Leute zuzugehen und auch unfreundlichen Gästen gegenüber freundlich zu sein. Aber es gibt Tage, da ist 60 es schon stressig."

Wegen der Abschlussprüfungen an der Realschule musste Susanne weniger Stunden machen, damit die Arbeit als Kellnerin ihre Schulnoten nicht beeinträchtigt. In der Tat 65 findet sie das Gegenteil: „In Kopfrechnen bin ich echt besser geworden", sagt sie lachend.

Auch Andreas Förthner arbeitet seit über zwei Jahren in direktem Kundenkontakt. In 70 einem Supermarkt räumt er zweimal pro Woche die Regale ein oder ist in der Getränkeabteilung für [1]das Leergut zuständig. Seine Eltern finden es schon gut, dass sich der 18-jährige Gymnasiast sein 75 eigenes Geld verdient. „Sein Bruder hat diesen Job früher immerhin auch einmal gemacht und mit der Schule hat es bislang auch keine Probleme gegeben", sagen sie.

<u>„Ich weiß genau, wo man alles im</u> 80 <u>Supermarkt finden kann und welche</u> <u>Flaschen wir zurücknehmen dürfen", sagt</u> <u>Andreas. Wenn Kunden genervt und</u> <u>unfreundlich sind, hat er seine eigene Taktik</u> <u>entwickelt: „Man muss sympathisch sein und</u> 85 <u>den Kunden helfen."</u>

Die Arbeit macht ihm Spaß und er verdient ja gut damit, aber vor allem ist sich Andreas über eines im Klaren: „Es ist eine gute
90 Erfahrung. Man bekommt ein anderes Gefühl fürs Geld und überlegt sich, wofür man es ausgibt; aber lebenslang möchte ich das auch nicht machen."

[1]**das Leergut = the empties**

QUESTIONS

Marks

1. Why do many young people find that they need a part-time job?   **2 points**

2. Sebastian Herbst is one of these students.

   (*a*) What exactly does he do?   **1 point**

   (*b*) What **two** major expenses does he want to pay for?   **1 point**

   (*c*) How did he come by his job?   **1 point**

3. Read lines 29–42.

   (*a*) How does Sebastian organise his work?   **2 points**

   (*b*) What comment does he make about the weather?   **1 point**

   (*c*) What **two** things does Sebastian say about his job?   **1 point**

Now read lines 43–61.

4. (*a*) What motivated Susanne Hupfer to find work?   **1 point**

   (*b*) Why did she particularly want to be a waitress?   **1 point**

5. What does Susanne say about dealing with people?   **2 points**

6. Read lines 62–68.

   (*a*) Why is Susanne working fewer hours just now?   **1 point**

   (*b*) In what way has her job helped her at school?   **1 point**

7. Read lines 69–79.

   (*a*) What does Andreas' job involve?   **2 points**

   (*b*) Why do his parents have no objections to his working?   **2 points**

8. Read lines 87–93.

   Why does Andreas feel his job has been a good experience?   **1 point**

9. Translate into English: **(20 points)**

                                         = 20 marks

   „Ich weiß genau, . . . den Kunden helfen." (lines 80–86)   **10**

                                             (30)

[Turn over for SECTION II on *Page four*

SECTION II—DIRECTED WRITING

Marks

You recently took part in an exchange visit to Germany. One day your host family took you on a trip to a town some distance away.

On your return to Scotland, you send in an article **in German** for the newspaper of your exchange partner's school.

You must include the following information and **you should try to add** other relevant details:

- who all were in your host family and what their home was like

- what the family's local area was like and what there was to do there

- how the family spent a typical day

- what you did on the day you went on this special trip

- what you all did for food that day

- whether you would recommend the experience of an exchange trip to someone else.

Your report should be 150 – 180 words in length.

Marks will be deducted for any area of information that is omitted. **(15)**

[END OF QUESTION PAPER]

X060/303

NATIONAL
QUALIFICATIONS
2006

WEDNESDAY, 24 MAY
11.00 AM – 12.00 NOON

GERMAN
HIGHER
Listening Transcript

This paper must not be seen by any candidate.

The material overleaf is provided for use in an emergency only (eg the recording or equipment proving faulty) or where permission has been given in advance by SQA for the material to be read to candidates with additional support needs. The material must be read exactly as printed.

SCOTTISH
QUALIFICATIONS
AUTHORITY

> **Instructions to reader(s):**
> The dialogue below should be read in approximately 3 minutes. On completion of the first reading, pause for two minutes, then read the dialogue a second time.
>
> Where special arrangements have been agreed in advance to allow the reading of the material, those sections marked **(m)** should be read by a male speaker and those marked **(f)** by a female.

Katherina, a 21 year-old German who is studying in Scotland, talks about issues concerning a healthy lifestyle.

(m) **Ist für dich die Gesundheit wichtig?**

(f) Ja, die Gesundheit ist für mich sehr wichtig. Ich denke, dass Jugendliche fit sein sollten, damit sie auch noch gesund bleiben, wenn sie älter sind.

(m) **Was machst du denn, um fit zu bleiben?**

(f) Ich gehe regelmäßig mit meiner Freundin zusammen joggen, nehme am Badminton-Unterricht teil und spiele zweimal die Woche Volleyball.

(m) **Und passt du auf, was du isst ?**

(f) Ja, ich denke schon. Ich würde jetzt nicht jeden Tag zu McDonalds gehen oder mich von Fastfood ernähren, sondern achte schon darauf, dass ich viel Salat und Gemüse esse.

(m) **Ist Fastfood denn bei euch in Deutschland genauso beliebt wie hier in Schottland?**

(f) Ich denke, in Deutschland gehen weniger Leute zu McDonalds oder Burger King, aber hier in Schottland habe ich festgestellt, dass ganz viele Familien mit jungen Kindern sich von Fastfood ernähren.

(m) **Und apropos gesundes Essen, haben deine Eltern in dieser Sache immer ein gutes Beispiel gegeben?**

(f) Meine Eltern haben immer sehr darauf geachtet, dass wir jeden Tag viel Obst und nicht zu viel Süßigkeiten gegessen haben.

(m) **Und wie oft trinkst du Alkohol?**

(f) Ich trinke manchmal am Wochenende. Ab und zu ein Bier, aber nicht sehr regelmäßig.

(m) **Und gibt es ein Alkoholproblem in Deutschland?**

(f) In den Großstädten gibt es sicherlich ein Problem mit Alkohol. Aber ich denke, nicht mehr oder weniger als hier in Schottland. Ich glaube, das ist ziemlich gleich.

In Deutschland können die Jugendlichen schon mit 16 Bier oder Wein trinken und diese Getränke auch legal im Laden oder in einer Kneipe kaufen.

(m) **Wie steht's denn mit dem Rauchen? Das passt doch nicht zu einem gesunden Leben, oder?**

(f) Nein, Rauchen ist natürlich sehr ungesund. Ich selber rauche nicht und habe nie geraucht. Viele Jugendliche rauchen aber, weil es cool ist; Gruppenzwang—dann raucht man eben zusammen mal eine Zigarette. Ich denke, das ist in allen Ländern gleich.

(m) **Gibt es Unterschiede zwischen Schottland und Deutschland bezüglich der Gesundheit?**

(f) Ja, es gibt große Unterschiede. Es ist mir aufgefallen, dass sehr viele Menschen in Schottland zu dick sind und Gesundheitsprobleme haben, auf Grund ihres Gewichts. Hier sehe ich auch kleine Kinder, die sehr dick sind und keinen Sport treiben können. In Deutschland ist das nicht der Fall, meiner Meinung nach.

(m) **Woran liegt das?**

(f) In deutschen Schulen essen die meisten Kinder in der Pause ein Butterbrot oder einen Apfel, und man darf in der Schule keine Süßigkeiten verkaufen. Hier in Schottland sehe ich in den Pausen ganz viele Kinder mit Chipstüten herumstehen. So was kommt in Deutschland nicht vor. Und fast jedes Kind treibt auch am Nachmittag Sport, denn bei uns gibt es viele Sportvereine für Jugendliche.

[END OF TRANSCRIPT]

[BLANK PAGE]

FOR OFFICIAL USE

Examiner's Marks

A	
B	©

Total Mark

X060/302

NATIONAL
QUALIFICATIONS
2006

WEDNESDAY, 24 MAY
11.00 AM – 12.00 NOON

GERMAN
HIGHER
Listening/Writing

Fill in these boxes and read what is printed below.

Full name of centre

Town

Forename(s)

Surname

Date of birth

Day Month Year   Scottish candidate number   Number of seat

Do not open this paper until told to do so.

Answer Section A **in English** and Section B **in German**.

Section A

Listen carefully to the recording with a view to answering, **in English**, the questions printed in this answer book. Write your answers **clearly** and **legibly** in the spaces provided after each question.

You will have 2 minutes to study the questions before hearing the recording.

The recording will be played **twice**, with an interval of 2 minutes between the two playings.

You may make notes at any time but only in this answer book. **Draw your pen through any notes before you hand in the book.**

Move on to Section B when you have completed Section A: you will **not** be told when to do this.

Section B

Do not write your response in this book: **use the 4 page lined answer sheet**.

You will be told to insert the answer sheet inside this book before handing in your work.

You may consult a German dictionary at any time during **both** sections.

Before leaving the examination room you must give this book to the invigilator. If you do not, you may lose all the marks for this paper.

SCOTTISH
QUALIFICATIONS
AUTHORITY

SA X060/302 6/4370

Section A

Marks

Katherina, a 21 year-old German who is studying in Scotland, talks about issues concerning a healthy lifestyle.

1. Why does Katherina think that young people should keep fit?   **1 point**

2. What does Katherina do to keep fit?   **2 points**

3. In what ways does Katherina watch what she eats?   **2 points**

4. What differences concerning fast food does Katherina notice between Germany and Scotland?   **2 points**

5. How did Katherina's parents make sure she ate healthily?   **2 points**

Marks

6. How often does she drink alcohol? **1 point**

7. (*a*) To what extent does Katherina think there is an alcohol problem in Germany? **1 point**

    (*b*) What is the law in Germany with regard to alcohol and young people? **2 points**

8. What does Katherina say about smoking? **2 points**

9. What health issues has she noticed in Scotland? **2 points**

10. Why does Katherina think that children in Germany are not as overweight as many in Scotland? **3 points**

(20 points)

= 20 marks

[Turn over for Section B on *Page four*

Marks

Section B

Und du, ist für dich die Gesundheit wichtig? Passt du darauf auf, was du isst und trinkst? Was hältst du von Alkohol und Zigaretten?

Schreibe 120 – 150 Worte zu diesen Fragen!

10

(30)

USE THE 4 PAGE LINED ANSWER SHEET FOR YOUR ANSWER TO SECTION B

[END OF QUESTION PAPER]

[BLANK PAGE]

Official SQA Past Papers: Higher German 2007

X060/301

| NATIONAL QUALIFICATIONS 2007 | WEDNESDAY, 30 MAY 9.00 AM – 10.40 AM | GERMAN HIGHER Reading and Directed Writing |

45 marks are allocated to this paper. The value attached to each question is shown after each question.

You should spend approximately one hour on Section I and 40 minutes on Section II.

You may use a German dictionary.

SCOTTISH QUALIFICATIONS AUTHORITY

©

SECTION I—READING

Read this magazine article carefully then answer **in English** the questions which follow it.

This article is about Germans who are thinking about or are actually living in Australia.

Wie ist es wirklich, fern der Heimat zu leben?

Immer mehr Deutsche wollen nach Australien. Ulrich Blos, zum Beispiel, träumt seit sechs Jahren von Australien. „Ich habe hier in Deutschland eine gute
5 Arbeit", sagt er, aber seit er 2001 eine Weile auf einer australischen Farm gearbeitet hat, hat er diesen Traum. „Wir sind im Busch gewandert. Da war nur Wald, nur Natur, so weit das Auge reicht. Deutschland ist mir
10 jetzt zu eng. Es gibt zu viel Stress und Leistungsdruck. Ob und wann wir tatsächlich nach Australien gehen, weiß ich noch nicht. Vielleicht, wenn die Kinder erwachsen sind."

15 Marie Merkel ist Krankenschwester in *Berlin*. „Mit meinen Qualifikationen habe ich in Australien gute Chancen. Ich würde natürlich meine dreijährige Tochter mitnehmen. Mit vier Jahren könnte sie dort
20 in die Schule gehen." Eigentlich gibt es für sie nur eine Hürde: die hohen Kosten für die Visa und den beruflichen Qualifikations-Test. Insgesamt würde es wohl etwa 2000 australische Dollar kosten und so viel Geld
25 hat sie nicht.

Gerhard Scheller hat seinen deutschen Pass abgegeben und ist jetzt stolz darauf, australischer Staatsbürger zu sein. Gerhard und seine Frau Britta haben sich kennen
30 gelernt, als sie in *Hamburg* Informatik studierten. Seit 1994 leben sie in einem Vorort von *Sydney*. Zurückkehren wollen sie nicht: Er begann in Australien mit einem eigenen Betrieb, seit sieben Jahren fährt er
35 Trucks. Sein Fotoalbum erzählt eine Geschichte vom selbst ausgebauten Haus mit Garten, von schönen Tagen am Meer und Festen mit Freunden. „Der Anfang kann einsam sein, wenn man stumm in der Ecke
40 sitzt und nicht einmal Witze auf Englisch verstehen kann", sagt Gerhard. „Und um mit Australiern reden zu können, muss man etwas über Politik, Sport und Humor in Australien wissen."

45 „Und noch etwas sollten künftige Auswanderer bedenken", sagt Gerhard: „Es

kostet sehr viel Geld und Zeit, wieder nach Deutschland zu kommen. Wir waren erst nach acht Jahren das erste Mal in der Lage, für vier Wochen nach Deutschland zu 50 fliegen." Gerhards Fotos erzählen auch von der harten Arbeit hinter dem australischen Traum. Oft arbeitet er sechs Tage die Woche. „Ich habe noch nie in meinem Leben so lange und so hart gearbeitet. Keine 55 Mittagspause trotz 40 Grad im Schatten—die Leute hier arbeiten einfach weiter. Der Lohn ist geringer als in Deutschland und die Lebenshaltungskosten in *Sydney* viel höher." Was vermisst er an 60 Deutschland? Gerhard lacht. „Currywurst. Die bekomme ich hier nirgendwo." Heimweh kann auch die Form einer Wurst annehmen.

Für Antje Eildermann ist Australien ein 65 Geruch und ein Lachen. „Es riecht hier oft wochenlang nach Rauch", sagt Antje, die vor zwei Jahren von *Berlin* nach *Sydney* gezogen ist. Der Rauch kommt ab August von den Waldbränden in den Blue Mountains. Das 70 Lachen stammt von einem Vogel. Es ist der Ruf des Kookaburra, eines australischen Vogels, der hier überall vorkommt. Eigentlich wollte Antje gar nicht auswandern, sondern kam nach dem 75 Studium zum Praktikum. „Dann habe ich Marcel getroffen, geheiratet und bin geblieben." Manchmal vermisst sie Deutschland—„nicht das Land, eher den Alltag, den [1]Tchibo um die Ecke oder so, 80 aber ich liebe *Sydney*. Die Menschen sind sehr offen, man knüpft schnell Kontakte."

„Das Schulsystem finde ich aber nicht so gut," sagt Antje. „Gute Schulen sind in Australien in der Regel privat und relativ 85 teuer." Noch haben die beiden keine Kinder, „aber wenn wir Kinder bekommen, sollten sie eher in Deutschland zu Schule gehen", sagt sie. Es gibt diesen Plan, nach *Berlin* zurückzuziehen. „Mein Mann würde 90 mitkommen, er liebt Deutschland und war schon oft da", sagt sie. Sie möchte auch aus

beruflichen Gründen zurückkehren. Ihre
Eltern haben eine Firma in *Berlin*, die Antje
95 eines Tages übernehmen möchte. „In drei
bis fünf Jahren," sagt Antje, „werden wir
nach Deutschland auswandern." Vielleicht
wird sie dann eines Tages, auf dem Weg zum

[1]Tchibo, einen eingebildeten Feuergeruch
wahrnehmen und ein Lachen vermissen. 100
Heimweh ist ein vielseitiges Gefühl.

[1]Tchibo = a shop selling a brand of German coffee

QUESTIONS

Marks

1. (a) What experience made Ulrich Blos start dreaming about a life in Australia? **1 point**

   (b) How does he feel about Germany now? **2 points**

   (c) When might he go to Australia to live? **1 point**

2. Read lines 15–25.

   (a) Why is Marie Merkel thinking about moving to Australia? **2 points**

   (b) What is the only thing that is stopping her from going? **1 point**

3. Read lines 26–44.

   What does Gerhard Scheller say about starting a new life in Australia? **2 points**

4. Now read lines 45–64.

   (a) What do Germans thinking of emigrating to Australia need to be aware of, according to Gerhard? **1 point**

   (b) What information does Gerhard give about his working life? Mention **three** things. **3 points**

5. Read lines 65–82.

   (a) What sums up Australia as far as Antje Eildermann is concerned? **2 points**

   (b) Antje never intended to emigrate. Why did she stay in Australia? **1 point**

   (c) What does she like about people in Sydney? **1 point**

6. Read lines 83–101.

   (a) What does Antje say about schools in Australia? **1 point**

   (b) Why will they probably return to Berlin one day? **2 points**

   (20 points)

   = 20 marks

7. Translate into English:

   „Gerhard Scheller hat . . . Vorort von *Sydney*." (lines 26–32) **10**

   (30)

[Turn over for SECTION II on *Page four*

SECTION II—DIRECTED WRITING

Marks

You have travelled to Germany to spend a holiday with German friends of your parents. While you are there, you are asked to baby-sit one day from 3.00 pm until 8.00 pm.

When you return to Scotland, you have to write a report **in German** for the Languages department in your school/college.

You must include the following information and **you should try to add** other relevant details:

- what the journey to Germany was like and how you felt travelling on your own

- who all was in the family and what they were like

- where the family house was situated and what it was like

- how you spent the five hours with the children while their parents were out

- what you did usually on your other evenings while in Germany

- why you would/would not baby-sit for this German family again.

Your report should be 150 – 180 words in length.

Marks will be deducted for any area of information that is omitted.

(15)

[END OF QUESTION PAPER]

X060/303

NATIONAL
QUALIFICATIONS
2007

WEDNESDAY, 30 MAY
11.00 AM – 12.00 NOON

GERMAN
HIGHER
Listening Transcript

This paper must not be seen by any candidate.

The material overleaf is provided for use in an emergency only (eg the recording or equipment proving faulty) or where permission has been given in advance by SQA for the material to be read to candidates with additional support needs. The material must be read exactly as printed.

SCOTTISH
QUALIFICATIONS
AUTHORITY

©

Instructions to reader(s):

The dialogue below should be read in approximately 4 minutes. On completion of the first reading, pause for two minutes, then read the dialogue a second time.

Where special arrangements have been agreed in advance to allow the reading of the material, those sections marked **(m)** should be read by a male speaker and those marked **(f)** by a female.

Candidates have two minutes to study the questions before the transcript is read.

Nicole, a German-language assistant, is interviewed about her Abitur and what she did after the exams.

(m) **Nicole, du hast letztes Jahr Abitur gemacht. Wie war diese Zeit für dich?**

(f) Ja, ich habe letzten Mai Abitur gemacht. Das war eine sehr stressige Zeit. Wir hatten wahnsinnig viel zu tun. Es gab viel zu lernen, viele Bücher zu lesen und Aufsätze zu schreiben. Ich hatte damals sehr viel Stress; ich erinnere mich noch ganz gut an alles.

(m) **Wie hast du dich darauf vorbereitet—also auf das Abitur?**

(f) Wir haben einen Lernplan gemacht, um den ganzen Stoff unterzubringen. Wir haben von Woche zu Woche verschiedene Sachen gelernt und das immer wiederholt. Ich hatte überhaupt keine Freizeit mehr. Ich konnte meine Freunde nicht mehr so oft treffen und hatte fast keine Zeit mehr, Sport zu machen. Und ja, die Zeit war einfach sehr knapp.

(m) **Und wie ist das Abitur gelaufen?**

(f) Es ist gut gelaufen. Ich war sehr zufrieden mit meinen Noten; ich hatte einen Durchschnitt von 1,5, was sehr gut ist.

(m) **Was habt ihr nach dem vielen Stress gemacht, um zu feiern?**

(f) Wir haben drei bis vier Tage nur Party gemacht. Außerdem hat die Schule eine große Feier organisiert—mit der ganzen Jahrgangsstufe.

(m) **Und als Belohnung hast du was gemacht?**

(f) Ja, dann sind wir in Urlaub auf die Insel Fuerteventura gefahren. Wir sind eine große Clique von ungefähr zehn Leuten und wir hatten diesen Urlaub schon länger geplant. Es gab viel zu planen—die Flüge, die Unterkunft und die ganzen Unternehmungen—und das war unsere Belohnung für das Abi.

(m) **Wie habt ihr die Reise organisiert?**

(f) Wir haben das per Internet gemacht und haben uns Informationen aus dem Reisebüro geholt.

(m) **Lief alles nach Plan?**

(f) Ja, eigentlich schon. Aber es sind drei Leute verhindert gewesen. Corinna konnte nicht mitgehen—wegen ihrer Eltern. Sie haben es ihr verboten. Mario konnte nicht mit; er hatte eine Arbeit gefunden. Und eine Freundin von mir—Nadine—wurde krank. So konnte auch sie nicht mitgehen. Aber ansonsten lief alles nach Plan.

(m) **Und habt ihr Spaß auf der Insel gehabt?**

(f) Ja, es war cool—super. Wir hatten viel Spaß. Wir sind viel weggegangen. Wir haben am Meer in der Sonne ausgespannt und wir haben eigentlich eine Woche gar nichts gemacht —ein paar Ausflüge am Tag, einige Sehenswürdigkeiten angeschaut—wirklich richtig locker und ohne Stress.

(m) **Ihr habt das Abitur richtig gefeiert, ja? Würdest du das weiterempfehlen?**

(f) Ja, ich würde es auf jeden Fall weiterempfehlen. Es war eine sehr, sehr schöne Zeit. Und die Erholung im Urlaub hat man sich dann richtig verdient. Es ist auch die letzte Gelegenheit, mit den Freunden so viel Zeit zu verbringen, bevor man auf die Uni geht oder eine Arbeit sucht. Und deshalb würde ich es weiterempfehlen, die Zeit einfach zu genießen und viel mit Freunden zu unternehmen.

[END OF TRANSCRIPT]

[BLANK PAGE]

FOR OFFICIAL USE

Examiner's Marks	
A	
B	

Total Mark

X060/302

NATIONAL QUALIFICATIONS 2007

WEDNESDAY, 30 MAY 11.00 AM – 12.00 NOON

GERMAN HIGHER Listening/Writing

Fill in these boxes and read what is printed below.

Full name of centre

Town

Forename(s)

Surname

Date of birth

Day Month Year

Scottish candidate number

Number of seat

Do not open this paper until told to do so.

Answer Section A **in English** and Section B **in German**.

Section A

Listen carefully to the recording with a view to answering, **in English**, the questions printed in this answer book. Write your answers **clearly** and **legibly** in the spaces provided after each question.

You will have 2 minutes to study the questions before hearing the dialogue for the first time.

The dialogue will be played **twice**, with an interval of 2 minutes between the two playings.

You may make notes at any time but only in this answer book. **Draw your pen through any notes before you hand in the book.**

Move on to Section B when you have completed Section A: you will **not** be told when to do this.

Section B

Do not write your response in this book: **use the 4 page lined answer sheet.**

You will be told to insert the answer sheet inside this book before handing in your work.

You may consult a German dictionary at any time during **both** sections.

Before leaving the examination room you must give this book to the invigilator. If you do not, you may lose all the marks for this paper.

SCOTTISH QUALIFICATIONS AUTHORITY

Section A

Marks

Nicole, a German-language assistant, is interviewed about her Abitur and what she did after the exams.

1. What made Nicole's Abitur so stressful?

   2 points

2. (*a*) How did she prepare for the exams?

   1 point

   (*b*) How did this affect her free time?

   2 points

3. How did she do in her Abitur?

   1 point

4. What celebrations followed the exams?

   2 points

5. (*a*) Nicole's reward was a holiday on Fuertaventura. With whom did she go?

   1 point

   (*b*) What did they have to plan?

   2 points

DO NOT
WRITE IN
THIS
MARGIN

Marks

5. **(continued)**

    (*c*) How did they go about organising their trip?   **1 point**

6. In what way did things not quite go according to plan?   **3 points**

7. How did they spend their time during the holiday?   **3 points**

8. Why would Nicole recommend doing something like this with friends?   **2 points**

(20 points)
= 20 marks

[Turn over for Section B on *Page four*

Marks

Section B

Und du, was hast du vor, diesen Sommer nach den Prüfungen zu machen? Fährst du mit den Eltern oder Freunden in Urlaub oder musst du einen Job finden?

Schreibe 120 – 150 Worte zu diesen Fragen!

10

(30)

USE THE 4 PAGE LINED ANSWER SHEET FOR YOUR ANSWER TO SECTION B

[END OF QUESTION PAPER]

[BLANK PAGE]

[BLANK PAGE]

[BLANK PAGE]

[BLANK PAGE]

[BLANK PAGE]

Acknowledgements

Leckie and Leckie is grateful to the copyright holders, as credited, for permission to use their material.

The following companies have very generously given permission to reproduce their copyright material free of charge: Gruner & Jahr AG & Co KG for the article 'Jobhopping' from *Young Miss Magazine* (2004 Higher Paper pp 2-3); Heinrich-Bauer Zeitschriften Verlag KG for the article 'Maria, 18 "Ich bin shopping-suchtig"', taken from *Magazine: Bravo Girl* No. 21, September 2003 (2005 Higher paper pp 2-3).

Pocket answer section for
SQA Higher German
2004–2007

© 2007 Scottish Qualifications Authority, All Rights Reserved
Published by Leckie & Leckie Ltd, 3rd Floor, 4 Queen Street, Edinburgh EH2 1JE
tel: 0131 220 6831, fax: 0131 225 9987, enquiries@leckieandleckie.co.uk, www.leckieandleckie.co.uk

Higher German
Reading and Directed Writing
2004

SECTION I – READING

1. (a) • she would become a tax consultant
(like him)
tax / financial adviser
accountant
she would follow him into his career
she would do the same job as him
she would follow his model as a tax
consultant
she would model herself on him and become
a tax consultant

(b) • friend **offered** her job in **furniture** shop /
store / company / business
friend **offered** her a job in the **furniture**
business as a saleswoman
OR
friend **offered** her job in **his** / **their** business

2. • to sample / try out various / different areas /
types of work
to try a wide range of jobs
to try practical work and jobs in different fields
to sniff out / nose around in various types of job
to spend time in different jobs
through practice and jobs in various occupations

• to test (out) herself and her talents (for different
jobs)
to bring out her talent(s)
to try and find her talent(s)
to discover / find out what she was talented at
to see what she is good at
thereby testing her talents to see what suits her
best
to see what she is good at
until she finds one that suits her
until she found the right one

3. • figures / balance sheets were not for her
business management was not for her
she does not like figures etc / numbers and
balancing
she did not want to do business management any
longer

• she would study/do French and Spanish /
languages
She wanted to do a language(s) course
She travelled home and started to study French
and Spanish at Cologne University because she
does not like Business Management = 2 points

4. (a) • exciting (line of) business / work
lots of things happening
OR
to see / find out / discover if this would be
the job for her

(b) • (too many) problems with grammar
she was struggling with grammar
she found the grammar very hard

5. (a) **Any 2 from the following:**

• she would see foreign countries
she would see lots of places
she would travel a lot / all round the world
she gets to see countries she has not seen

• she would **constantly/always/continuously**
experience new things
continual new experiences

• (she would be) working with people
having to do with people
have a lot to do with people
dealings with people

(b) • they were not (very) enthusiastic
with little enthusiasm
they had / were filled with little enthusiasm
they did not think much of it
less than / hardly enthusiastic
they weren't exactly enthusiastic
they were hardly filled with enthusiasm
OR
eventually they accepted their daughter's
decision
ultimately they just had to trust her choice
in the end

6. (a) **Any 2 from the following:**

• seen a lot of countries / places and improved
her languages / her speaking in the foreign
language / her language skills
she has seen a lot of the world and improved
her language skills

• **she** has become **more** flexible
she is now **more** flexible

• she knows / understands what good service is
/ means

Higher German
Reading and Directed Writing
2004 (cont.)

6. *(b)* • she could / would not get any more out of
this job
she could not learn / improve any more from
this job
there's nothing more to get out of the job
you can't get any more out of the / this job
OR
it was time for something new / a new start /
beginning
she needed a new job / a fresh start
a new start was in order
she had to find something new
it was time for a new start / to move on
she wanted to start something new
she needed a new job
time for a new start

7. *(a)* • she got a permanent / steady / regular / stable
job / post / position
they offered her a permanent post

(b) • she (tele)phones / calls a lot / often /
frequently / regularly
she uses the phone a lot

• good / strong / real / close / true / deep
friendships survive separation / last despite
the distance
she thinks that distance does not matter with
good friendships
deep friendship can survive / last over
distance
OR
good relationship with parents survives
distance

8. *(a)* • she does not need / have to be rich
she does not think she has to be rich
she is not interested in money
she does not care about money

(b) • being / remaining a journalist for a long while
she cannot see herself moving for a long time
sees her future in journalism
wants to continue her career in journalism
enjoying journalism / journalism is for her
she has found her ideal job in journalism
she will stick to the job she has
she is happy and contented in this job
she will complete her training as a journalist

• she can / could see / imagine herself **opening**
a café
she could / might **open** a café
she smiles / jokes about **opening** a café
perhaps she'll **open** a café

9. Mona uses / used / utilised / made use of the time
(left) (up) until / (leading) up to / till her first flight
for her fourth job experiment. She sells / sold
children's clothes / clothing / childrenswear /
kidswear / kids' clothing in a (department) store.
What she learns / learned there above all (other
things) / above everything else / more than
anything / most of all is team-work, working hand
in hand with others / with other people / how to
work hand in hand with others. That was a very /
really important experience for her.

SECTION II – DIRECTED WRITING

Please refer to **2007 German Reading and
Directed Writing** Section II – Directed
Writing. The table on pages 11-12 details what
is required to produce a good essay answer.

Higher German
Listening/Writing
2004

SECTION A

1. (a) • twice a week
two days a week

  (b) • woman / mother alone / on her own **during the week**
  mother spends week alone
  father is away **during the week / all week**
  husband / father **works** away from home
  husband **must work** in **Frankfurt**

  • woman has three **small / little / young** children
  youngest child five months old
  one is five months old

2. (a) **Any 2 from the following:**

  • playing with the children

  • helping with the meal(s)
  help prepare the food / meals / dinner / lunch
  make meals
  cooks the food
  feeds the children

  • bath the children
  gives children a bath
  washes the children

  • puts the children to bed
  gets children ready for bed

  (b) • €5 **per hour**
  5 euros **per hour**

3. **Any 2 from the following:**
  • parents give her pocket money **every month**
  she gets it **monthly**
  monthly / every month

  • € 30 paid/put into her **bank** account

  • € 15 given in cash / for her(self) / in her pocket
  she gets € 15 to spend (on what she likes)
  she gets € 15 directly from her parents

4. (a) • clothes **and / or** things for school
  clothes **and / or** school stuff / things / equipment
  clothes **and / or** school books / stationery
  Both must be mentioned

  (b) • when she goes out
  for a meal **out** / to buy food **when she goes out**
  for eating **out**
  when she is going (out) to the cinema
  for the cinema

  (c) • they / grandparents / family live / stay (too) far away
  they live further away
  they live away from her
  they do not stay in the area
  they do not live near(by) / here

5. **Any 2 from the following:**

  • plays basketball **in / for a club / team**
  she is in a basketball team

  • she **is meant** to train 3 times a week
  during the term she trains once a week
  she does not do it so often when she has schoolwork
  she trains more in the holidays

  • (during the season) plays in games against other clubs
  plays games / matches against other teams
  they have matches against other teams

6. (a) **Any 2 from the following:**

  • you can book them by phone
  you can call them up and book / order
  you can call them any time
  you just phone up

  • they take you (right) to your home / house / front door
  they drop off you off at your house
  it is practical to use them to get home in the evening
  • the last one leaves at **1.10**
  it's on / they run until **1.10**

  (b) • she gets the taxi cheaper
  Sammeltaxis are cheaper with bus pass
  it costs less / it is cheaper / it does not cost as much
  it saves her money on taxis
  you don't have to pay as much
  (Sammel)taxi / it only costs € 1.20
  € 1.20 – very cheap / much cheaper

7. (a) **Any 2 from the following:**

  • she sends e-mails to friend(s) in Florida / Australia
  she contacts / talks to

  • when sister **was** in Italy, Lisa in contact with her / Lisa e-mailed her / chatted with sister in Italy
  (daily) contact with sister, when sister **was** in Italy

  • can e-mail her family **from / while in** Scotland

  (b) • **she** does not play / like (computer) games
  she does not use it for games

  • computer available for schoolwork
  always free when people want to use it
  always free when she wants / needs to use it
  it's not used most of the time

SECTION B

Please refer to **2007 German Listening/Writing** Section B. The table on pages 14–15 details what is required to produce a good essay answer.

Higher German
Reading and Directed Writing
2005

SECTION I – READING

1. **Any two of:**
    - she feels like a star/celebrity
      she feels as if the red carpet has been rolled out for her
      she feels as if the red carpet is going to be rolled out for her
    - her eyes (start to) shine/light up/sparkle/gleam/glisten/glitter/glint
      her eyes become bright
    - her heart beats/pumps/goes fast**er**
      her heart rate increases
      her heart races
    - she has/gets butterflies in her stomach/tummy/belly
      she gets butterflies

2. **Any two of:**
    - she wants clothes like the pop singers she sees on TV
      she wants to look like the pop singers she sees on TV
      she sees pop singers on TV in their cool clothes and goes out to buy clothes like that/those clothes
    - a **voice in her head** tells her to buy things/shop
      a **voice in her head** is egging her on
    - she **wants** to be/look attractive/beautiful/pretty/popular/ loved

3. they made fun of/mocked her
    they joked and bitched about her
    they made jokes/nasty/snide remarks about her
    they made jokes etc. about her masses of shopping bags
    or
    she withdrew/drifted away from them
    she pulled back from them
    she drew/stood back/moved away from them
    she became isolated/detached from them
    she is no longer in that group

4. **Any three of:**
    - she got **money** from her grandparents/grandma/grandpa
    - she borrowed/got a loan of money
      she was lent money/she asked for a loan/she got a loan
    - she **asked her family** for money at Christmas/birthdays
      she would wish for money from her parents at ...
      she wanted money from her parents at ...
    - she took money from her savings account
      she began to spend money from her savings account
      she started eating into her savings
      she raided/ate into her savings
      she stole from her account

5. (a) the more she had/earned, the more she spent/bought/went shopping
       since/as she had more, she spent more
       she spent/shopped even more
       her spending really took off

    (b) they thought it was good that she was learning to handle/deal with money/budget
       they wanted her to learn to handle/manage money
       to let her learn how to handle money
       they wanted her to learn her way round money
       they wanted her to learn how to use money properly
       they wanted her to learn money management
       they wanted her to learn responsibility with money
       their daughter had to learn to handle money

6. (a) (sometimes) she did not know/had no idea/sense of how much she **had spent**

    (b) • they depressed her/she was/felt/became depressed
         they weighed her down/troubled her deeply/more and more
       • she suffered/spent sleepless nights
         she lost sleep at night/could not sleep (at night)
         she had trouble sleeping
       • she couldn't see herself living a normal life
         she saw herself without the/any possibility/opportunity of a normal life
         she saw herself with/she worried about the possibility of not leading a normal life
         she wondered if she could/will lead a normal life
         if she stays like this, she will be without the possibility of leading a normal life

7. (a) she banned herself from going to town/stayed away from the town/imposed a city ban on herself/prescribed herself a town ban or went out without any money/took no money with her when she went out (both elements required)

    (b) window-shopping **and** made lists of/wrote down things to buy
       or
       made lists of/wrote down things to buy **and** when she had money
       She would go window-shopping and make a list of all the things she wanted to buy
       She wrote lists of the things she wanted to buy when/if/as soon as she had money (again)/so she could come back when she had money/with the money

8. **Any two of:**
    - she burst/broke into tears/was crying a lot/was frequently tearful/would start to cry
    - she was nervous/jittery/edgy/**looking** anxious
    - she began to/would shake/tremble/shake/quiver/got the shakes/she was caught trembling
    - she couldn't concentrate/lacked/lost concentration

9. • she does not borrow (money)
     she has stopped borrowing money
     she does not get her friends to lend her money
     any more
     she does not get loans from her friends
   • she has paid back almost/nearly/practically
     everything/most of it
     she has paid back most of what she
     borrowed/owes
     she has paid back most of her debts
     she has paid almost all of them back
     she has returned nearly everything

10. My parents told me that I should go to the doctor.
    And that was the best thing that could have
    happened to me. The doctor spent a long time
    talking to me. For the first time I spoke quite
    openly about my shopping addiction.

SECTION II – DIRECTED WRITING

Please refer to **2007 German Reading and
Directed Writing** Section II –
Directed/Writing. The table on pages 11-12
details what is required to produce a good essay
answer.

Higher German
Listening/Writing
2005

SECTION A

1. (*a*) • trains/training twice
       • one or two games/matches etc.
       • he plays once or twice
       • game/match once or twice

   (*b*) • once a fortnight/every fortnight
       • once every two weeks
       • every second week(end)/fortnight/two weeks
       • every other weekend
       • every two weekends
       • twice a month

2. **Any two of:**
   • boys' appearance matters to girls
     girls think it is important how boys look
     girls like boys who look good
   • To gain a point here, candidates must refer
     clearly to boys **looking** fit/sporty etc.
     girls like a boy with a sporty
     physique/figure/shape
     girls like boys who look fit/are in good shape
     girls like boys with an athletic/muscular figure
     girls like fit guys because they have a
     nicer/better body
     girls are attracted to a sporty figure
   • girls find a fat boyfriend embarrassing
     fat/fatter people are unattractive
     girls don't want a fat boyfriend
     girls don't like fat guys

3. **Any two of:**
   • watches sports programmes on TV
     watches sport on TV
     watches (favourite) sport (programme) on
     Saturdays
   • reads sports magazines
   • plays table-tennis – **with his brother**
     plays table-tennis **when he has time**

4. (*a*) going to go out/away **more** (often)
       (hopes) to go out **more** (often)
       allowed out **more** (often)

   (*b*) at a dance/dance-hall/club/disco
       dancing/clubbing
       or
       in/at an ice-cream parlour/at an (ice-)café

5. he is the (only) goalkeeper
   or
   he has a responsibility/duty towards the team/the
   others
   he does not want to let the team down
   he owes it to the team/he has to be there for his
   team
   he is committed to his team
   he is answerable to his team
   or
   his girlfriend/she would/should/will understand
   he would expect girlfriend to understand
   girlfriend will be understanding

Higher German
Listening/Writing
2005 (cont.)

6. (a)
- he would miss/cancel/drop/skive off training.
  he would miss a training session
  he would cut back on his training
- once a fortnight
  every two/second/other weeks

(b) cut back on her hobby/one of her interests
do something similar/the same for him
give up something she does/a hobby (for him)
give up something as well
sacrifice her hobby/hobbies
make sacrifices (for him)
compromise on her hobbies

7.
- she/they will/would understand if he does not have time (at weekend)
  understanding if/when he has no time (at weekend)
  she would understand at weekends
  more understanding why he has to go to training
  they would understand if he was too busy
  they would understand his sporting commitments
- she might come to the odd game
  she might come to a match from time to time
  she might come and watch him play
  she could support his team

8.
- not/no more than twice a week
  maximum of twice a week
- Saturday **evening/night**

9. (a) each/every day/daily/on a daily basis

(b)
- they forget (about) everything else
  they forget everything around them
  they forget about things/the world around them
  they forget everything apart from each other
- should not abandon/drop/forget friends/team **because of a girl/relationship/and only focus on the girlfriend/just to spend time with a girlfriend/and let your relationship take over your life/over a girl**
  love life should not interfere with your sport
  girlfriends are not as important as the team

SECTION B

Please refer to **2007 German Listening/Writing** Section B. The table on pages 14-15 details what is required to produce a good essay answer.

An underlining indicates that a particular word or idea must be present in the answer for the answer to be acceptable eg <u>Friend's</u> <u>birthday</u> (party) – separate underlinings of "Friend's" and "birthday" indicate that the candidate must show understanding not only that this was a <u>birthday</u> party, but that the party was for a <u>friend</u>.

By similar token, a phrase such as "<u>from all over Europe</u>" should be underlined as a phrase (and not as single words, ie "<u>from</u> <u>all</u> <u>over</u> <u>Europe</u>"), as it is the phrase and not the individual words which are important.

Higher German
Reading and Directed Writing
2006

SECTION I – READING

1. *Any two of:*
- their life is expensive
  being a student/a young person is expensive
  they need money for: 2 of their phone, clothes, the cinema, holidays
- pocket money (usually) not enough
  pocket money does not cover their costs
  the money they get from their parents is not enough/insufficient/inadequate
- so that they do not have to rely on parents
  so that they can earn their own money
  so that they do not need to go to their parents
  it is a welcome alternative to the parental purse
  to stop taking money from their parent's purse/pocket

2. (*a*)
- delivers/distributes <u>TV (guides) and other magazines/illustrated papers</u>
  OR delivers magazines/papers/does a paper-round <u>twice a week</u>
  OR delivers/distributes magazines/papers/does a paper-round <u>on his bike</u>

(*b*)
- <u>exchange/school</u>-trip to France <u>and</u> trip/journey/holiday/travel to Scotland

(*c*)
- mother saw/read advert in the paper
  mother found the job/it in the paper
  mother showed him the ad in the paper
  his mum read about it in the newspaper

3. (*a*)
- divides his round into 3
  divides the area into 3 rounds
  does it in 3 trips
  he shares it between 3 tours
  in 3 tours of the district
- does one round after the other (on his bike)
  does each in turn

3. (*b*)
- has to go out in all weathers/no matter the weather/he has to work in any weather conditions
  customers want their magazines in all weathers/despite the weather
  OR
- it is awful/difficult/bad/not good/rubbish/silly/stupid/a pain when it is hot/there is (black) ice
  it seems stupid when it is hot/there is (black) ice

(*c*) *Any two of:*
- easy money
- fun/likes doing it/enjoys his job
- does not interfere with his school work/school work does not suffer/school work can fit around it

4. (*a*)
- financial independence/freedom
  she was financially dependent/she is financially independent

(*b*)
- because of the hourly rate/pay/wages <u>and</u> tips
  good pay <u>and</u> tips

5. *Any two of:*
- every customer/guest is different/the work is varied
- she finds working/dealing/getting on with people easy/the contact with people is easy for her
  she finds it easy to relate to people
- you learn to approach people in a relaxed way
  you learn to be relaxed with/around/towards people
  you learn to be cool with people
- (you learn) to be friendly/nice/pleasant towards unfriendly/unkind people/guests/customers/clients
- some days/sometimes/at times/there are days when it is/can be stressful/can cause a lot of stress

6. (*a*)
- because of her school leaving/end of school/final exams
  so her work doesn't affect her marks/grades/results/exams
  she does not want her school grades affected
  so she does not spoil her school grades
  so that work does not impair/get in the way of her school grades
  she has to concentrate on her grades
  to get the grades she wants
  to get her grades

Higher German
Reading and Directed Writing
2006 (cont.)

6. (b) • she's improved her mental arithmetic
she is better at mental arithmetic/sums in
her head/working things out in her
head/counting in her head/calculating in
her head
with mental arithmetic

7. (a) *Any two of:*
• direct contact with the public/customers
• fills/stacks the shelves/fills the empty
shelves
• in charge of/responsible for the empties in
the drinks department

(b) *Any two of:*
• it's good/nice he is earning money
they are pleased he is earning money
• his brother did same job before/once/
earlier
his brother had the/this/that job
• there have been no problems with school
it did not affect his/their schooling
the job gave his brother no problems with
school

8. *Any one of:*
• you have a different/new attitude towards
money
you have a different feel(ing) for money
you feel differently about money
you have another feeling for money
you get a new feeling for money
you get a better understanding of money
you get a better sense about money
you get a different outlook on money
it has given him an appreciation of the
value of money
• you think about/consider how you spend
your money/what you spend it on/what
you buy with it
you spend it in a more considered way
you are more careful with money/you take
more care with money
• he would not want to do this for ever/life
he would not want to do this job all his
life/his whole life

9. „Ich weiß genau, wo man alles im Supermarkt
finden kann
*I know exactly/precisely/the exact place where you
can find/one/people can find everything in the
supermarket/all the things in the
supermarket/anything in the supermarket/where
everything can be found in the supermarket*

und welche Flaschen wir zurücknehmen dürfen",
sagt Andreas.
*and which/what bottles we are allowed/permitted
to/may take back/accept says/said Andreas*

9. (continued)

Wenn Kunden genervt und unfreundlich sind,
*If/When/Whenever customers/clients are
irritated/worked up/annoyed/stressed and
unfriendly/unpleasant*

hat er seine eigene Taktik entwickelt:
*he has developed/he has worked out/he has devised/
his own strategy/strategies/tactics/tactic*

„Man muss sympathisch sein und den Kunden
helfen."
*You/One must be/have to be/need to be
pleasant/nice/congenial and help the
customers/clients/be helpful to the customers/provide
help for the customers.*

SECTION II – DIRECTED WRITING

Please refer to **2007 German Reading and
Directed Writing** Section II –
Directed/Writing. The table on pages 11-12
details what is required to produce a good essay
answer.

Higher German Listening/Writing 2006

SECTION A

1. • so that they are healthy/healthier/fit when they are older/old/adults/in later life/in the future
   so that they aren't unhealthy when they are older

2. *Any two of:*
   • goes jogging/running with friend(s)
   OR goes jogging/running regularly
   • gets/goes to/takes badminton lessons
   • plays volleyball twice a week

3. • would/does not go to McDonalds/fast food restaurants every day/daily
   does not go to McDonalds much/regularly/very often
   does not eat fast food every day
   rarely/seldom eats fast food/McDonalds
   does not eat much/a lot of fast food
   would/does not live off fast food
   avoids/keeps clear of fast food
   eats a limited amount of fast food
   • eats a lot/plenty of salad and vegetables

4. • few(er)/not (as/so) many/less/not a lot of Germans go to fast food restaurants
   • Scotland/Britain/here – (lots of) families with young/small/little children eat/live on fast food/go there
   young families go there

5. • (a lot of) fruit each/every day/daily
   • not too/so many/much/not a lot of sweets/sweeties/candy/confectionery

6. • sometimes + at the weekend
   now and again/then + at the weekend
   from time to time + at the weekend
   occasionally + at the weekend
   not very often + at the weekend
   not regularly + at the weekend
   every so often + at the weekend
   some weekends

7. (a) • there is a problem in cities/big(ger) towns/in the city
   no more or less than in Scotland
   it is much the same as in Scotland
   no better or worse than in Scotland
   it is pretty much equal to Scotland
   not any great difference between Scotland and Germany

   (b) • can drink/buy beer or wine at 16 (in pub)
   • can buy it in shop at 16

8. *Any two from:*
   • it is unhealthy/bad for your health
   it is bad for you
   • she does not smoke/never has smoked (and never will)
   • (lots of) young people/teenagers do it because it is/looks cool
   young people do it to look cool
   • people smoke due to peer pressure

9. • a lot of/(too) many people are too fat
   a lot of people have health problems because of weight/they are fat
   • little/small/young children who are very/really/too fat/really overweight/obese
   there are (some) very fat small children
   some small children are very fat
   little/small/young children who cannot/are unable to do sport because of their size/because they are so fat

10. *Any three of:*
    • German children/they eat a sandwich/bread (and butter)/roll/apple at the interval/at break
    Germans take a sandwich to school
    • sweets not sold in schools (in Germany)
    you cannot buy sweets in schools
    • Scots eat crisps at break time/at school
    In Scotland they eat crisps at break time/at school
    Germans do not eat crisps at school
    • (German) children do sport in the afternoon/after school/after lunch
    almost every German child does sport
    lots of sports clubs for them

SECTION B

Please refer to **2007 German Listening/Writing** Section B. The table on pages 14-15 details what is required to produce a good essay answer.

Higher German
Reading and Directed Writing
2007

SECTION I—READING

1. (a) He worked on a farm in Australia (in 2001)

   (b) *Any two of*
   - It is cramped/limited/crowded/packed/enclosed/not open enough/restricting/constricting/claustrophobic/limiting
     he feels confined and closed in/it feels too small
   - too much stress/too stressful
   - too much pressure to succeed/achieve/perform/work hard/do well

   (c) when the children are older/grown-up/adults
   when the children grow up

2. (a)
   - <u>with her qualifications</u> she has/will have....
     .. good prospects/opportunities/chances in Australia... a good chance of succeeding/doing well/getting a job in Australia... a good/greater/better chance in Australia
     Her qualifications as a nurse could be wanted in Australia
   - her daughter can/could start school at (age of) four
     in a year her daughter will be able to start school in Australia

   (b) she does not have the money/the 2000 dollars....
   ....for a visa and the test she'd have to sit
   the cost/expense of the visa and test she would have to sit

3. *Any two of*
   - it/you can/could/might be lonely
     it is sometimes lonely
   - (when you are) sitting <u>quietly/silently</u> in a corner
   - you cannot understand <u>jokes</u>/one <u>joke</u> in English
   - to speak to Australians you need to know/learn about Australian/their politics/sport/humour

4. (a) high cost <u>and</u> time needed to return to Germany
   it costs/takes a lot of time and money to go/get back to Germany/to visit Germany
   it costs/takes a lot of time and money to come (back) from Australia

   (b) *Any three of*
   - <u>often</u> works six days a week
   - has never worked so hard/so long/such long hours in his life
   - no lunch/dinner/midday break even in 40 degree heat
   - pay/wages/money/salary is less <u>than in Germany/at home</u>
     wages are low compared with Germany

5. (a)
   - the smell of smoke/it smells of smoke
   - the laugh/call/cry of the kookaburra/a bird

   (b) met and married Marcel/met her husband/met someone and got married

   (c) their openness/they are (very) open
   it is easy to get to know them/make contact with them/you make acquaintances quickly/you make/form contacts quickly

6. (a) the school system is not so/very good
   good schools are generally/mostly/usually/normally/mainly/(very) often/predominantly/as a rule private and expensive

   (b)
   - she wants her children to go to school in Germany/a German school
   - Antje will/wants to take over/take on/run her parents' business/firm/company in Berlin

7. „Gerhard Scheller hat seinen deutschen Pass abgegeben"
   Gerhard Scheller has given up/in/back
   gave up/in/back
   has handed in/over/back
   handed in/over/back his German passport

   „und ist jetzt stolz darauf, australischer Staatsbürger zu sein."
   and is now proud of/about being
   to be an Australian citizen/national

   „Gerhard und seine Frau Britta haben sich kennen gelernt"
   Gerhard and his wife Britta met
   got to know each/one other
   came to know each other

   „als sie in Hamburg Informatik studierten."
   when/whilst they studied/did
   they were studying/doing computing science/computer science/IT/Information Technology/Information Systems/Information Science in Hamburg.

   „Seit 1994 leben sie in einem Vorort von Sydney."
   Since 1994 they have been living/they have lived in a suburb of Sydney/Sydney suburb.

SECTION II—DIRECTED WRITING

Category	Mark	Content	Accuracy	Language Resource – Variety, Range, Structures
Very Good	15	• All bullet points are covered fully, in a balanced way, including a number of complex sentences. • Some candidates may also provide additional information. • A wide range of verbs/verb forms, tenses and constructions is used. • Overall this comes over as a competent, well thought-out account of the event which reads naturally.	• The candidate handles all aspects of grammar and spelling accurately, although the language may contain some minor errors or even one more serious error. • Where the candidate attempts to use language more appropriate to post-Higher, a slightly higher number of inaccuracies need not detract from the overall very good impression.	• The candidate is comfortable with almost all the grammar used and generally uses a different verb or verb form in each sentence. • There is good use of a variety of tenses, adjectives, adverbs and prepositional phrases and, where appropriate, word order. • The candidate uses co-ordinating conjunctions and subordinate clauses throughout the writing. • The language flows well.
Good	12	• All bullet points are addressed, generally quite fully, and some complex sentences may be included. • The response to one bullet point may be thin, although other bullet points are dealt with in some detail. • The candidate uses a reasonable range of verbs/verb forms and other constructions.	• The candidate generally handles verbs and other parts of speech accurately but simply. • There may be some errors in spelling, adjective endings and, where relevant, case endings. • Use of accents may be less secure. • Where the candidate is attempting to use more complex vocabulary and structures, these may be less successful, although basic structures are used accurately. • There may be minor misuse of dictionary.	• There may be less variety in the verbs used. • The candidate is able to use a significant amount of complex sentences. • In one bullet point the language may be more basic than might otherwise be expected at this level. • Overall the writing will be competent, mainly correct, but pedestrian.
Satisfactory	9	• The candidate uses mainly simple, more basic sentences. • The language is perhaps repetitive and uses a limited range of verbs and fixed phrases not appropriate to this level. • In some examples, one or two bullet points may be less fully addressed. • In some cases, the content may be similar to that of good or very good examples, but with some serious accuracy issues.	• The verbs are generally correct, but basic. • Tenses may be inconsistent, with present tenses being used at times instead of past tenses. • There are quite a few errors in other parts of speech – personal pronouns, gender of nouns, adjective endings, cases, singular/plural confusion – and in the use of accents. • Some prepositions may be inaccurate or omitted e.g. I went the town. • While the language may be reasonably accurate in three or four bullet points, in the remaining two control of the language structure may deteriorate significantly. • Overall, there is more correct than incorrect.	• The candidate copes with the past tense of some verbs. • A limited range of verbs is used to address some of the bullet points. • Candidate relies on a limited range of vocabulary and structures. • Occasionally, the past participle is incorrect or the auxiliary verb is omitted. • Sentences may be basic and mainly brief. • There is minimal use of adjectives, probably mainly after "is" e.g. The boss was helpful. • The candidate has a weak knowledge of plurals. • There may be several spelling errors e.g. reversal of vowel combinations.

Higher German
Reading and Directed Writing
2007 (cont.)

Category	Mark	Content	Accuracy	Language Resource – Variety, Range, Structures
Unsatisfactory	6	• In some cases the content may be basic. • In other cases there may be little difference in content between Satisfactory and Unsatisfactory. • The language is repetitive, with undue reliance on fixed phrases and a limited range of common basic verbs such as *to be, to have, to play, to watch*. • While the language used to address the more predictable bullet points may be accurate, serious errors occur when the candidate attempts to address the less predictable areas. • The Directed Writing may be presented as a single paragraph.	• Ability to form tenses is inconsistent. • In the use of the perfect tense the auxiliary verb is omitted on a number of occasions. • There may be confusion between the singular and plural form of verbs. • There are errors in many other parts of speech – gender of nouns, cases, singular/plural confusion, spelling and, where appropriate, word order. • Several errors are serious, perhaps showing mother tongue interference. • There may be one sentence which is not intelligible to a sympathetic native speaker. • One area may be very weak. • Overall, there is more incorrect than correct.	• The candidate copes mainly only with the predictable language required at the earlier bullet points. • The verbs "was" and "went" may also be used correctly. • There is inconsistency in the use of various expressions, especially verbs. • Sentences are more basic. • An English word may appear in the writing or a word may be omitted. • There may be an example of serious dictionary misuse.
Poor	3	• The content and language may be very basic. • However, in many cases the content may be little different from that expected at Unsatisfactory or even at Satisfactory.	• Many of the verbs are incorrect or even omitted. • There are many errors in other parts of speech – personal pronouns, gender of nouns, adjective endings, cases, singular/plural confusion, word order, spelling. • Prepositions are not used correctly. • The language is probably inaccurate throughout the writing. • Some sentences may not be understood by a sympathetic native speaker.	• The candidate cannot cope with more than 1 or 2 basic verbs, frequently *had* and *was*. • The candidate displays almost no knowledge of past tenses of verbs. • Verbs used more than once may be written differently on each occasion. • The candidate has a very limited vocabulary. • Several English or "made-up" words may appear in the writing. • There are examples of serious dictionary misuse.
Very Poor	0	• The content is very basic OR • The candidate has not completed at least three of the core bullet points.	• (Virtually) nothing is correct. • Most of the errors are serious. • Very little is intelligible to a sympathetic native speaker.	• The candidate copes only with "have" and "am". • Very few words are correctly written in the foreign language. • English words are used. • There may be several examples of mother tongue interference. • There may be several examples of serious dictionary misuse.

Higher German Listening/Writing 2007

Section A

1. *Any two of*
- a lot/lots/(so) much/loads/a huge amount to learn/study/do/revise
  she had so much work to do for them
- a lot of/lots of/loads of/(so) many <u>books</u> to read
- essays to write

2. (*a*)
- She had a revision/study/learning plan/programme
  She made a timetable for learning/a revision timetable
  OR
- She studied/learned new/different things/stuff/topics each week
  She studied something else/new things each week

(*b*) *Any two of*
- She did not have any (free time)/She had none.
  No (more) free time.
  It took away her free time
  Her time was all taken up
- Could not see/meet/go out with her friends as/so often/ as/so much
- Hardly any time for sport
  Practically/almost no time for sport
  She did hardly any sport

3.
- She was pleased/happy/satisfied/content with her mark(s)/ grade(s)/result(s)
  She thought she had done very well.
  OR
- she got (an average of) 1.5

4.
- 3 to 4 days/3 or 4 days of parties/partying
  They had a party/partied for 3 or 4 days/3 to 4 days
  There was a 3-4 day party
- (People from) school organised/had/held/threw/arranged (big)"do"/event/party/celebration/dance/ceremony

5. (*a*) a big/large group/crowd/clique of friends/pals
  (about) 10 friends/pals
  10 of her friends/pals

(*b*) *Any two of*
- the flight(s)/plane(s)
  the plane journey/ticket(s)
- accommodation/somewhere to stay
  where to spend the night
- activities
  what (they were going) to do
  everything/things to do

5. (*c*)
- internet/websites <u>and</u> travel agent/bureau/office
- booked it on-line <u>and</u> got info from the travel agent

6. *Any three of*
- three of the group could not go/make it three people pulled out
- one – could not go because of parents
  one – because of her parents/because her parents banned her
  Corinna's parents would not let her go
  Corinna was not allowed to go
- one – could not go because of work
  Mario found/got a job/had to work
- one – could not go because of illness
  Nadine took ill

7. *Any three from*
- went out a lot
- relaxing by the sea/on the beach/relaxing in the sun/by the sea in the sun (Answer must have 2 elements of relax+sea+sun.)
- spent a week doing nothing (at all)
- went on a couple/few/some excursions/(day)trips/outings
- did some sightseeing/saw the sights/went to see the sights

8.
- Last chance/opportunity/time to spend time with/to be with/to see your friends
- before going to university or starting a job
  before university or work/job.

Section B

Category	Mark	Content	Accuracy	Language Resource - Variety, Range, Structures
Very Good	10	• The topic is covered fully, in a balanced way, including a number of complex sentences. • Some candidates may also provide additional information. • A wide range of verbs/verb forms and constructions is used. There may also be a variety of tenses. • Overall this comes over as a competent, well thought-out response to the task which reads naturally	• The candidate handles all aspects of grammar and spelling accurately, although the language may contain some minor errors or even one more serious error. • Where the candidate attempts to use language more appropriate to post-Higher, a slightly higher number of inaccuracies need not detract from the overall very good impression.	• The candidate is comfortable with almost all the grammar used and generally uses a different verb or verb form in each sentence. • There is good use of a variety of tenses, adjectives, adverbs and prepositional phrases and, where appropriate, word order. • The candidate uses co-ordinating conjunctions and subordinate clauses throughout the writing. • The language flows well.
Good	8	• The topic is addressed, generally quite fully, and some complex sentences may be included. • The candidate uses a reasonable range of verbs/verb forms and other constructions.	• The candidate generally handles verbs and other parts of speech accurately but simply. • There may be some errors in spelling, adjective endings and, where relevant, case endings. • Use of accents may be less secure. • Where the candidate is attempting to use more complex vocabulary and structures, these may be less successful, although basic structures are used accurately. • There may be minor misuse of dictionary.	• There may be less variety in the verbs used. • Most of the complex sentences use co-ordinating conjunctions, and there may also be examples of subordinating conjunctions where appropriate. • At times the language may be more basic than might otherwise be expected at this level. • Overall the writing will be competent, mainly correct, but pedestrian.
Satisfactory	6	• The candidate uses mainly simple, more basic sentences. • The language is perhaps repetitive and uses a limited range of verbs and fixed phrases not appropriate to this level. • The topic may not be fully addressed. • In some cases, the content may be similar to that of good or very good examples, but with some serious accuracy issues.	• The verbs are generally correct, but basic. • Tenses may be inconsistent. • There are quite a few errors in other parts of speech – personal pronouns, gender of nouns, adjective endings, cases, singular/plural confusion – and in the use of accents. • Some prepositions may be inaccurate or omitted e.g. I go the town. • While the language may be reasonably accurate at times, the language structure may deteriorate significantly in places. • Overall, there is more correct than incorrect and there is the impression overall that the candidate can handle tenses.	• The candidate copes with the present tense of most verbs. • A limited range of verbs is used. • Candidate relies on a limited range of vocabulary and structures. • Where the candidate attempts constructions with modal verbs, these are not always successful. • Sentences may be basic and mainly brief. • There is minimal use of adjectives, probably mainly after "is" e.g. My friend is reliable. • The candidate has a weak knowledge of plurals. • There may be several spelling errors e.g. reversal of vowel combinations.

Section B (cont.)

Category	Mark	Content	Accuracy	Language Resource - Variety, Range, Structures
Unsatisfactory	4	• In some cases the content may be basic. • In other cases there may be little difference in content between Satisfactory and Unsatisfactory • The language is repetitive, with undue reliance on fixed phrases and a limited range of common basic verbs such as *to be, to have, to play, to watch*. • While the language used to address the more predictable aspects of the task may be accurate, serious errors occur when the candidate attempts to address a less predictable aspect. • The Personal Response may be presented as a single paragraph.	• Ability to form tenses is inconsistent. • In the use of the perfect tense the auxiliary verb is omitted on a number of occasions. • There may be confusion between the singular and plural form of verbs. • There are errors in many other parts of speech – gender of nouns, cases, singular/plural confusion – and in spelling and, where appropriate, word order. • Several errors are serious, perhaps showing mother tongue interference. • There may be one sentence which is not intelligible to a sympathetic native speaker. • Overall, there is more incorrect than correct.	• The candidate copes mainly only with predictable language. • There is inconsistency in the use of various expressions, especially verbs. • Sentences are more basic. • An English word may appear in the writing or a word may be omitted. • There may be an example of serious dictionary misuse.
Poor	2	• The content and language may be very basic. • However, in many cases the content may be little different from that expected at Unsatisfactory or even at Satisfactory.	• Many of the verbs are incorrect or even omitted. • There are many errors in other parts of speech – personal pronouns, gender of nouns, adjective endings, cases, singular/plural confusion – and in spelling and word order. • Prepositions are not used correctly. • The language is probably inaccurate throughout the writing. • Some sentences may not be understood by a sympathetic native speaker.	• The candidate cannot cope with more than 1 or 2 basic verbs, frequently "has" and "is". • Verbs used more than once may be written differently on each occasion. • The candidate has a very limited vocabulary. • Several English or "made-up" words may appear in the writing. • There are examples of serious dictionary misuse.
Very Poor	0	• The content is very basic.	• (Virtually) nothing is correct. • Most of the errors are serious. • Very little is intelligible to a sympathetic native speaker.	• The candidate copes only with "have" and "am". • Very few words are correctly written in the foreign language. • English words are used. • There may be several examples of mother tongue interference. • There may be several examples of serious dictionary misuse.

Official SQA answers to ISBN 978-1-84372-555-8
2004–2007